This book belongs to:

....

....

Made in the USA
Las Vegas, NV
30 July 2022

52300229R00085